The Coaching Handbook

150 Powerful Questions for Life Coaching and Personal Growth

Tim Hanson

Table of Contents

Introduction

Chapter 1: Personal Growth Questions

Chapter 2: Relationship Questions

Chapter 3: Fun Questions

Chapter 4: Health Questions

Chapter 5: Career Questions

Chapter 6: Money Questions

Chapter 7: Physical Location Questions

Conclusion

Recommended Life Coaching Books

SPECIAL BONUS

Copyright 2014 by Globalized Healing, LLC - All rights reserved.

Introduction

The ability to ask powerful, open-ended questions is the most brilliant tool that we as humans can possess. They don't have to be earth shattering or ground breaking questions that leave listener's with their jaw hanging down to the ground, although they can be. More importantly they need to be questions that will stimulate emotion to provoke "aha" moments; one's that leave the person in deep thought to inspire creativity, increase productivity, and blast glaring headlights on personal development.

Questions are the primary way to build a connection and develop lasting, meaningful relationships. They have brought peace in to broken, confusing relationships; they have helped to solve life's most complicated problems; and most importantly they've brought a deeper level of understanding to humanity so that society as a whole can give and get more out of life.

The questions you are about to embark upon will be ones that will open many doors that you once believed were locked with ten deadbolts. They will be ones for you to guide others to finding out what makes them tick – not like a time bomb but instead like a grandfather clock on the wall waiting to strike midnight.

You will find the book is divided into the eight important categories so that you can immediately jump to the section as needed.

Let's begin!

Chapter 1: Personal Growth Questions

Coach, Listen, and Be Curious

Coaches have been recognized as leaders in creating powerful questions to evoke transformation. Coaches' seek out to be leaders in personal development and business development. They get lit up to inspire, build, and connect with others, all of which begin with questions to determine what the other person *really* wants out of life.

Although questions are the primary focus of this ebook, it is important to understand that listening has equal importance in order for you to respond and create your own questions so that you can direct a conversation that will benefit the other person. Use the words they use to build other questions. For example, if a person says I don't like how things have changed, you can say "What do you mean by change? Can you give me an example?" This leads to further conversation and the conversation to get deeper, leading to more meaningful places.

Everyday of life we learn something new. Whether it be talking with a friend about his new born baby, watching the news to learn about a massacre in Iraq, or realizing that we like to listen to the acoustic version of Led Zeppelin. We learn things about events in the world, ourselves, and facts about life everyday when we listen.

Listening with our ears, observing things with our eyes, and listening to the inner sense of intuition are simple examples of ways to listen and understand.

One more thing before we dive into the questions is that the best questions come from being curious, non-judgemental, and keeping an open-mind to allow the door to be wide-open to possibilities.

This section was created with ways for both you and the person whom you are speaking with to gain purpose, understand oneself, and others in deeper, more meaningful ways.

- What do you want in life?

- What is your dream?

- What is your purpose?

- What else?

- In 1 month from now, where do you want to be? 3 months? 6 months? 1 year?

- What are you searching for?

- How will it feel to be there?

- What are you grateful for?

- Who do you want to be?

- What does that look like?

- What is important to you?

- Why is that important to you?

- Who do you admire or what type of person do you look up to? If he/she could offer you advice, what would it be?

- What are you 3 of your best qualities that you can bring to the situation?

- Tell me more.

- Imagine how it would feel once you accomplish this.

- What is getting in the way of living the life you want to live?

- Why do you want to be like this?

- What will this bring you?

- What do you need to do to get there?

- What do you value in life?

- What's the challenge here?

- If you could do one thing everyday, something that excites you to get out of bed everyday, what would that be?

- What's stopping you?

- Where can you get that information?

- What are the 5 most important things in your life? What else do you want?

- What excites you and makes you feel alive?

- What makes you smile? How can you add more of that to your day? (to your life?)

- If you were to paint a picture of your life one year from now, what would it be?

- How have you changed from when you were 10 years old? 20? 30?

- If your life were to represent a color in this exact moment, what would that be? Why? What does this color mean to you?

- Imagine you were 95, what would you like to say about your life?

- Lets set a deadline. When do you want to accomplish this by?

- How will you know you have accomplished it?

Chapter 2: Relationship Questions

Relationships are the best part of life. Every relationship takes time and effort from both people and requires a level of understanding of why another person does the things he or she does. It is important to know what a person is looking for and wants out of the relationship. Both parties need to be benefiting or else the relationship will not last.

Therefore, these are the questions can be used to get to the bottom of what a person *really* wants in a relationship.

- What would you rate your current relationship on a scale of 1 to 10 (with 1 being terrible and 10 being excellent)?

- What do you like about your relationship?

- What do you want more of in your relationship?

- When you think of this relationship, how does it make you feel?

- What is something you've wanted to tell your partner, but have resisted due to fear?

- What do you want?

- What are the 3 most important qualities that the person must have?

- What are the 3 qualities that you can not stand in a partner?

- Can you see yourself with him/her 20 years from now?

- What do you want more of?

- What is the first step to getting more of what you want?

- What does your intuition say?

- Who are you in the relationship?

- What have you learned from your past (or current) relationship?

- What would your life be like if this person were to die tomorrow?

- What would you tell this person if you knew that today were his/her last day?

- Who do you have to be to attract this type of person?

- When do you want this by?

- Where do these type of people hang out? Where else?

- How would your best friend (or the person who knows and understands you best) describe you?

- Let's say a similar situation happens again, what will you do differently?

- Looking at the big picture, how important is this to you?

Chapter 3: Fun Questions

Life was meant to be fun – it is a necessity to life. We work in order to have fun and enjoy time with our selves and our families. Fun can range from things from relaxing on a couch and laughing at a sitcom on Television to having an adventure at an amusement park with our families.

This category was created to open doors to what a person wants for fun and how he can bring more fun into his or her life.

- What do you want more of in your life?

- What does fun mean to you? What else?

- If you had more fun in your life, how would that feel?

- When you are having fun, who so you see with you?

- On a Scale of 1 – 10 (with 10 being the highest), what do you rate the level of fun in your life today? Where do you want it to be tomorrow? One week from now? One month from now?

- How important is fun to you?

- When you were 10 years old, what was fun to you? What if you were to bring that feeling back into your life?

- What if we were to remove fun from your life? What would your life be like?

- If you had one day that was dedicated to having fun, what would you do?

- What is one thing you've always wanted to do, but haven't due to fear?

- How can you bring more fun into your life?

Chapter 4: Health Questions

Without health, we would not be alive. So of course health needs to be addressed. It is topic that needs to be addressed for the completion of the 7 categories of personal development.

- What does it mean to be healthy to you?

- What would you rate your current level of health on a scale on 1 to 10 (with 10 being excellent)? What do you want it to be?

- What would you look like if your health were a 10? How would you feel?

- What would your day look like if your health were a 10?

- What do you want to improve?

- What is possible?

- What else?

- Who will support you?

- What are the other options?

- What is best for you?

- What are the consequences of not improving your health?

- When do you want to accomplish this by?

- Why do you want this?

- If your life depended on taking action, what would you do today? Tomorrow?

- How will you know when your health is a 10?

Chapter 5: Career Questions

A persons' career can bring a huge amount of happiness (or sadness) to their life. Therefore, one needs to get clear on what it is that will make them happy (which is the primary goal of humans worldwide), as a large part of ones life will be spent working at a career you either love or hate.

- If you could do anything, and knew you couldn't fail, what would you do? Why?

- Who do you have to be (an adjective, or a real or fictional character) to get where you want?

- Who do you admire? What would he/she say to you right now?

- What is your greatest strength? How can you bring more of that to you current (or future) career?

- What are you passionate about? What things get you excited?

- Is money or job satisfaction more important to you?

- How do you believe that money and career are related? How does that apply to your life?

- What are you afraid of?

- Can you be more specific?

- What area do you need more clarity with?

- Who can you talk to in order to get more clarity on your decision?

- What would it feel like to be there (or have that career)?

- Let's set a deadline. When do you want this by?

Chapter 6: Money Questions

Money. It keeps the world going around. Money gives people the opportunity to travel, fulfill wants and needs, as well as provide for a family. The lack of it causes much pain and hardship. To some it is important above all things and to others it is toward the bottom of the ranking, below relationships, health, and career satisfaction.

This section will guide you with questions surrounding the field of money.

- If I were to give you 1 million dollars today, what would you do with it? How important is that to you? In one year from now, what will you feel about the way your money was spent?

- What are the possibilities?

- What are your fears (around money)?

- What do you need to say no to in your life in order to make more money?

- What do you need?

- What do you want to make more money for?

- Who do you want to make more money for?

- What will more money bring you?

- What's stopping you from achieving your financial goals?

- What mindset do you need to have to accomplish this?

- Who are you? Create a metaphor (e.g. I am the glorious money tree who attracts money and gives other what they need.)

- What does success mean to you?

- How will others perceive you if you reach your financial goals? Is that important to you?

- What will you need to do to achieve this?

- What are the consequences of not achieving your financial goals?

- What is the action plan?

- When will you have X amount of money by?

Chapter 7: Physical Location Questions

To some, the physical location matters above all. Some dream of being on the beaches of Hawaii, whereas others dream of being in the Mountains of Park City, Utah. If a person wants it bad enough, they will do whatever it takes to get there, and then start a life. It happens everyday. This section will help people get clear on this part of their life.

- What do you rate your level of happiness with your physical location (on a scale of 1- 10, with 10 being the highest)?

- Where do you want to be?

- If you could live anywhere – no restrictions, where would it be?

- Imagine your ideal location. What is around you (e.g. mountains, beach, farms)?

- What are the people like?

- Who else is there?

- What does you life look like on a daily basis?

- How important is it for you to get there?

- What is stopping you from getting there?

- What are you afraid of?

- What excites you?

- What's stopping you from getting there?

- How would you feel if you never achieved it?

- What do you need more of? What can you do to get it?

- When do you want to be there? How will it feel once you are there?

Chapter 8: Master Questions For Elaboration and More Coaching Questions

These are the questions to get more information out of people. Best of all, the information gathered will come from a place of curiosity as opposed to a place of judgement, so the person will be more likely to respond favorably. These questions often lead to places you never knew existed. They will boost conversations and keep them going for hours.

- What do you mean by that?

- Let's take an outside perspective. What does your life look like now?

- What is important about that?

- What does that mean to you?

- What is your perspective? What is another perspective?

- How do you see it?

- What would that look like?

- How do you feel about that?

- Can you tell me more?

- What's stopping you?

- What do you want from today's session?

- What is worse – failing or never trying?

- If you could offer a child one word of advice, what would it be?

- How can you bring more joy to your life?

- Are you living for yourself or for someone else?

- What other thoughts do you have about this?

- How else do you feel about this?

- Can you give me an example?

- What have you learned?

- So what's the advice here?

- Do you need a reminder? What can you use to remind yourself?

- One year from now, what will you think about today?

- Are you ready to make a commitment?

- Would you like me to hold you accountable?

- Where are you now (in the present moment)?

- What is the emotion here? Tell me about it.

- What's your body telling you? What are you noticing?

Conclusion:

Some say money makes the world go around but I believe questions make the world go around because without questions, there would be no money. It would be a world filled with assumptions and judgments, without taking ones point-of-view into account. It would be a world filled with confusion and a lack of clarity.

My request for you (if you haven't already) is to go out and use these questions everyday in your conversations. You will find more meaning in all of your relationships and get more clarity for your own and others' journey with personal development. Use the questions to get clear on what it is you truly want.

Use these questions to coach yourself and coach others to strengthen your relationships, improve your health, and advance your careers. I encourage you to look back on these questions, and review your previous answers to see your personal growth and progress.

Made in United States
Troutdale, OR
03/19/2025